40 Day
Mind Fast
Soul Feast

D0038604

40 Day
Mind Fast
Soul Feast

Dr. Michael Beckwith

Edited by
Anita Rehker

Agape Publishing
Culver City, California

Editor's Note

To those familiar with New Thought terminology, the meaning of "soul" is that subjective faculty which reflects back the forms of thought which are given it. In everyday parlance, this is the subconscious mind, that which is beneath the level of conscious awareness. Throughout this book, however, "soul" is defined as the indwelling Presence of God within each individual.

Foreword

It was one year ago at Morehouse College that the Rev. Dr. Michael Beckwith was inducted into the Dr. Martin Luther King, Jr. Order of Preachers. In a room of three thousand people, his light shone brightly. "Him I must meet," I promised myself.

Little did I know on that occasion that I was destined to be spiritually mentored by one of the contemporary mystics of our time. I made repeated pilgrimages to his Agape International Truth Center in Culver City, California. In a non-traditional sanctuary filled with thousands from diverse cultural, ethnic, racial and spiritual backgrounds, I heard him pronounce: "There is only One Power, One Presence, One Life, and It is the very Essence of your life. You *are* what you are looking for." His words resonated with such absolute conviction and clarity that I felt their truth reverberating within my consciousness long after they were uttered. With an ear acclimated to great orators from university lecterns and church pulpits alike, I recognized that I was in the presence of that rare individual who absolutely embodies that of which he speaks.

I say with complete confidence that as an undisputed forerunner of the New Thought-Ancient Wisdom teachings, Dr. Beckwith's commitment to his personal practice of these timeless truths makes him a worthy vehicle for pointing many souls in the direction of spiritual unfoldment. I find him to be firmly planted in the earthly and the sublime, which gives him a deep compassion and sense of playfulness so refreshing in a spiritual teacher.

My recent trip to India and Nepal with Dr. Michael—as he is affectionately called—was a revelation and a transformation into the nature of personal chaos, order and agape."Mind fasting" and "soul feasting" is an activity of consciousness that eases us into an understanding of the relationship of this transforming trinity existent within us. Filled with practical guidance, encouragement and affirmations, this book speaks to myriad aspects of the interior life encountered by the modern spiritual seeker. Through application of its wisdom, your life will provide compelling proof of your true nature: wholeness, peace, compassion and joy.

Lawrence Edward Carter, Sr.
Dean, Morehouse College Chapel
Professor of Philosophy and Religion

Introduction

The science of Quantum Physics has forever dissolved our rational, three-dimensional understanding of time and space, of energy and matter. It has proven that there are no random or accidental acts in the Universe. Dr. Carl Jung's theory of synchronicity describes an aspect of this principle. That you now hold this book in your hands is indeed by Divine Appointment, in accordance with synchronous Divine Right Timing.

This is a book about how to arrive at ultimate inner fulfillment, but it contains no information on how to get what you think you need to be happy or how to improve relationships in this world of effects. This book's purpose is to usher you into a soul awakening. In tune with your soul-nature, you will automatically demonstrate that realization of your oneness with God is the Source of your supply, joy and peace of mind.

One of the greatest spiritual scientists, lovers of God and humanity who graced our world is Jesus the Christ. His life and teachings proclaim that he was not an exception; rather, he is an example of how we are to live if we are sincere about our own spiritual awakening.

An experience of Jesus' that speaks to my heart is described in the fourth chapter of Matthew, the Temptation of Jesus. From a metaphysical viewpoint, the rite of purification Jesus underwent during his forty days and nights in the wilderness proved him to be a Self-realized being. He annihilated any sense of an egoic self, any sense of separation from the Godhead. Jesus knew he had the power to manifest bread to appease the hunger of his physical body, yet he claimed that he lived not by gross food, "but by every word that comes from the mouth of God." He spoke mystically, declaring that he lived directly from the Life Force that divinely sustains all creation. His second temptation was an invitation to put on display his spiritually illumined consciousness by commanding angels themselves to appear and protect him from bodily harm. Here he overcame the ego's desire for adulation, name and fame. Finally, during the third temptation to succumb to the allurement of owning worldly kingdoms, Jesus conquered the ego's love of materialism, the false sense of ownership of things belonging to this temporal world.

Every number held a significance to the ancients, and the number forty resounds throughout the Bible, specifically in connection with purification and spiritual triumph: Jesus' forty days and nights in the wilderness; Elijah fasted for forty days; the great flood of forty days and nights from which Noah was spared; Moses' forty days and nights on Mount Sinai conversing face-to-face with God. It took the Israelites forty years from the time they left Egypt until they arrived in Canaan.

I now invite you to set your own personal intention for a similar sojourn in consciousness. For the next forty days, ascend to the holy ground of your own being where the true Second Coming of the Christ Consciousness takes place. *When the consciousness that was in Christ Jesus is awakened within you, then you will be born again of the Spirit.* No longer will you wander in the wilderness of ignorance, drenched by the flood of the world's values, thinking you are separate from God, seeking for satisfaction in sources powerless to give it. Instead, you will live your life from a new plateau of consciousness, steeped in the love and wisdom of the Infinite.

Colors, like numbers, have their own vibrational qualities. Springing from Nature Itself, color has its origin in a higher reality. Blue represents the formless Substance of the Christ Consciousness pervading all creation. The field of the mystical third eye is blue. Since antiquity, blue has been used by the world's spiritual traditions in its iconography to represent a high state of spiritual consciousness. Mary's robe is depicted as blue; Lord Krishna's skin is blue; Islamic tiles have the same hue of deep blue as Christian stained glass windows.

Blue has been selected as the ink color for the pages of this book because of its equivalence with that which is Divine, so that the vibration of the Christ Consciousness may be roused in the reader's soul and heart.

As you prepare for the first day of your journey, know that you are entering a sacred tryst with the Spirit. Find a quiet place. Calm the body and inwardly prepare your consciousness by affirming your openness and receptivity. Breathe, and feel your heart area expand. With the eye of the soul, read Day 1. Attune your inward ear and listen as the Spirit speaks to you in the voice of your own inner guidance system. Repeat this process during each of the forty days.

Dear One, this is the beginning of your "mind fast" from the outer world, and your "soul feast" at the banquet table of your innermost being.

Peace and blessings,
Rev. Dr. Michael Beckwith

Day 1

*The Divine Plan is one of Freedom. The
inherent nature of man is ever seeking to
express itself in terms of freedom, because
freedom is the birthright of every living soul.*
Ernest Holmes

The Soul's Organic Freedom

There is a wise Zen saying that says you cannot
stop birds from flying around your head, but you
can prevent them from making nests in your hair.
As you begin to mature spiritually, you discover
that although you cannot stop the world's chatter
about lack and limitation from whirling around
you, you can prevent it from lodging in your
awareness. How? By actively practicing the
Presence of God, the compass of your mind develops
the habit of continuously turning in the direction of
the Spirit for intuitive guidance, comfort, security,
wisdom, joy, peace, truth and love.

I'm not suggesting that you should deny that
noisy birds of limitation sometimes fly around in
your experience, tempting you to throw them some
crumbs of your attention. What I am saying is that
by staying your attention on the Changeless
Reality of your God-Self, you will experience an
inner freedom from the things that distract you

from the truth of your divine nature.

There is a tendency in human nature to look to the external world for fulfillment that can only be found within. That which is merely external is powerless to satisfy the soul. By reversing the searchlight of your senses and focusing your attention on that which is Real, you will undergo a permanent shift in consciousness which will requalify your entire experience.

This day, set your intention to silently converse with the Spirit in the language of your heart. If it is peace that you seek, look first to the Source of peace sitting right on the altar of your own being. If it is joy for which you yearn, commune with its Source in meditation and prayer. Then, at the end of the day, you will see how you met the needs of each moment with God in your consciousness. You will be free from the intrusive clamor of mediocrity going on around you, and at last taste the freedom for which your soul yearns.

I am free as Spirit is free. I renounce any sense of being bound by habit, personal history, experience or circumstance. Wisely using the Law of Freedom, I walk free of all that would limit me.

Day 2

You can attract only that which you first mentally become and feel yourself to be in reality.
Ernest Holmes

Make a Commitment to Life!

Contemplate the truth that you and I stand as a midpoint between heaven and earth, with access to a nexus of Divine Creativity. Right now, you have not only the ability but also the responsibility to exercise your God-given freedom to live life at your highest level of creativity.

The moment you claim your ability to co-create with the Spirit, your human mind begins dissolving the false boundaries that previously kept you from consciously operating the Law of Co-creation. God has a gift to give to the world as you, beyond what your surface mentality may sometimes see. So when you commit to discovering and expressing your faculty of Divine Creativity, what emerges is living and expressing from a deeper dimension of your being. This is real aliveness. Then you may say with conviction, "Thou art the Doer, not I." You are catapulted into the realm of Truth and consciously co-create your life with the Christ of your being.

So shine your light that its effulgence imprints a glow of joy on your face that no external circumstance can erase. If you withhold your gifts from expressing in this world, there exists within you a sense of incompleteness; there is a feeling of not having arrived at your true purpose. You are an individualized expression of God, here to shine the light that lights up every man and woman who comes into the world. At every point in your incarnation you are being asked to reveal the Kingdom of God on earth as it is in heaven. Buddhism has a maxim: "Nobody is special." None of us is special, but each one of us is essential to the Divine Plan or we would not exist.

Today, before you leave your home to play your part in this world, fling open wide the portals of your consciousness in prayer, inviting That which created you in Its own image and likeness to reveal how you may breathe each breath and walk each step as a free agent of conscious co-creativity.

Today I commit myself to my divine destiny as a creative being. I know every path is open before me as I consciously co-create with the Spirit. I glow with the fire from heaven.

Day 3

Service, Not Servitude

"Stop working, start serving!" As this thought forcefully pressed in upon my consciousness, I was pulled within to converse with the Spirit. Why was this statement presented into the field of my awareness? As I placed myself in a listening mode, I began to understand that many people have the concept that they go to "work." Think of the new vocabulary that would emerge if the world embraced an attitude of service and generosity of the heart, rather than work! When you perform that which has been given you to do with an attitude of work, you are actually in servitude to that work. You are a servant to your own burdensome false idea. Service, on the other hand, is freedom.

Ralph Waldo Emerson said that we place the Universe in our debt as we give more than what we are compensated for, if we don't work for mere money alone. Since we cannot outgive the Self-givingness of the Spirit, the Universe will create opportunities to give even more back to us than we could ever give to it.

You are here to serve the great Law of Life. You are, in fact, in service to the Supreme Creative Idea that proliferates our environment. It is the Life of God that is thinking through your mind, working through your hands, walking through your feet. It does the work appointed for you to do and perfects that which concerns you when you no longer "work" for the little self, but "serve" the greater Self of your being and the Universe.

Today, recognize and practice—no matter what your job description is—that you are in service to an Eternal Idea. No task is too great or too small when done in loving service. Then you will joyfully act with detachment, surrendering the fruits of your labors to the Infinite. Open yourself to what the Hindus call *seva*, which means service, and you will find yourself filled with a Divine vitality and vigor that comes directly from the inexhaustible Font of Inspiration, which is the Eternal Idea Itself.

I know myself to be a Divine Center of loving and creative service. I give generously to life and am vitalized, energized and magnetized by the living Spirit.

Day 4

*What lies behind us and what lies before
us are tiny matters compared
to what lies within us.*
Ralph Waldo Emerson

Freedom's Testimony

I recently heard testimony from a woman whose history described her as a five-time felon confined to death row. Not surprisingly, she began to think about God, rather than the impending doom awaiting her. As her relationship with the Spirit deepened, it overtook her consciousness as being the Supreme Reality, and profound changes began to occur. At first, it was small things: she was allowed to exercise in the yard; she joined the prison choir and began to sing the good news about the Spirit. Eventually, her death sentence was reduced to a life sentence. Today she is free, and spends her time visiting churches singing and speaking about the empowering Presence of God.

The truth is that she became free the moment she turned to the Spirit within her own being as her refuge and strength. As she merged her mind with the One Mind, she sloughed off the sense of a self separate from the Essence of her life. Her union with God became so complete that she experienced a new incarnation right within this very lifetime. Divine Law responded, and everything around her conformed to a new birth in her true identity. She would have been free had she never left the confines of the prison cell because she was inwardly free already!

Many people give themselves death sentences served out in the prison of their own minds. They are prisoners of fear, jealousy, lack, limitation, greed and selfishness.

Today, examine the self-created prison into which you have confined yourself. Then, be willing to step into your God-consciousness without any thought of personal reward. Watch the shackles of your false beliefs, unwanted habits and negative thought patterns fall away as the revelation of your true Self unfolds. Desire freedom of the Spirit. Set your intention to live your life in the freedom consciousness that is already yours!

I claim the Truth that I was created free, born free and live in my true state of spiritual freedom. I feel, sense and know there is only a Law of Freedom and I am governed by it now.

*Believe. The promises of God are real. They
are as real, as solid, yes infinitely more solid
than this table which the materialist so
thoroughly believes in. If you would
only believe, O ye of little faith.*
George Washington Carver

Have Faith In Faith

When you have faith the size of a mustard seed and abandon yourself and all the details of your life to it, your greater-yet-to-be bursts forth. You will meet it everywhere. It will press itself against you and multiply around you! You will hear the Spirit whispering inwardly to you about why you are here and what you have come to do, revealing the agreements in your Divine Contract.

You don't have to wait for external circumstances to shift before such a transforming experience overtakes your life. Right now, on the ground on which you stand, you can breathe in the sublime, rarified atmosphere of the Holy Spirit. Then you will know absolutely that you live in a supportive Universe. There will be a tearing down of the strongholds of negativity. There will be the glory of the Living God moving through you in ways you can't even imagine. Be vigilant in your faith! It is your shield and your fortress. Those who practice faith walk freely everywhere they go in this world. No mental barbs of negativity can penetrate their interior armor of conviction that God is the Source and Substance of their supply, their Sustainer, Provider and Comforter.

For the remainder of your waking hours this day, participate in this spiritual experiment: Every hour on the hour, stop, take a deep breath, and give thanks for your life. Then move back into your daily rounds of activity with an awareness of the Eternal beating in your heart. As you do this, you will notice that this form of discipline causes you to remember who and what you really are. With repeated practice, your faith in your true identity creates space for you to no longer live in the past or future. Instead, you will be available, awake and alive in the Eternal Now.

I have faith in faith! My faith is active, unconditional, and everything in my experience conforms to this truth.

Day 6

The subliminal mind receives and remembers all those touches that delight the soul. Our soul takes joy in this right touching by the Essence of all experience.
Sri Aurobindo

The Touch of Anointing

When you move into your prayer life, into those moments of private time with the Spirit, that is when you contact the fulfilling Presence within you. Oftentimes you think you are going to God to change some condition in your life, to fulfill some material desire or need. What you really are going to God for is to capture a sense of spiritual fulfillment. When you truly tabernacle with the Spirit, the desire for anything less falls away!

Even when your intention in speaking your word is to manifest something material, if you touch the sacred Presence through Divine communion, you forget any external desire that first drew you into prayer! This is what is meant by right touching. As you reach within to touch consciousness, the Divine reciprocates by corresponding, by touching you with the hand of Divine Grace.

This makes it obvious why you would want to add to your spiritual discipline moments of agendaless prayer. In other words, there are times when you sit and just love God and all that God means to you. Having no other purpose than to be consumed by the Divine Energy of your prayer, you touch Spirit's vulnerability and experience the truth in scripture which says, "While they are yet praying I have already answered."

Agendaless prayer will transcend the surface tension of separation and let you become aware that it is God's good pleasure to give you the kingdom. You have now placed yourself in a position of receptivity; you have become gracious enough to accept the gift.

Today, set aside time that belongs only to you and God. Experiment with agendaless prayer in the laboratory of your consciousness and discover Spirit's personal love for you that is so great It personalized Itself as your very life.

I appreciate my Divinity and use it to manifest my soul's desire to realize my oneness with the Infinite. My heart opens to the Divine, Transforming Touch of the Godhead.

*The Unseen One, featureless, unthinkable,
undefinable by name, Whose Substance is the
certitude of One Self, in Whom world-exis-
tence is stilled, Who is all peace and bliss
—that is the Self, that is what must be known.*
Mandukya Upanishad

The Desire Beyond All Desiring

Often when people materialize things they don't
feel any closer to their God-Self than before the
object of desire appeared in their lives. Why?
Because this is materialization, not manifestation.
It's subtle, so don't allow yourself to be confused!
What you consistently dwell upon ultimately takes
shape as your experience. Consciously or uncon-
sciously, everyone can and does materialize.

In contrast, manifestation places you in league
with the Divine Spiritual Pattern of who and what
you are as a spiritual being. Manifestation is
accomplished through a clear realization of oneness with God. It brings in its wake the recognition
that God is the desire beyond all desiring.
Conscious union with the Spirit bestows the
manifestation of all needs met.

Spirit so loves to manifest that It placed Its own
Divine Light at the center of your being. At your
core, beyond the limiting thought forms you

temporarily may have bought into, there is a Divine Blueprint, a spiritual integrity factor. Today, dare to come out of the materialization mode and enter into the manifestation consciousness that is your birthright! In this state of consciousness, you live each moment as an embodiment of the words of Jesus when he said, "Strive first for the kingdom of God and his righteousness, and all these things will be given to you as well." Then the birds themselves will carry food to your doorstep.

I acknowledge only one desire in my consciousness: God alone! I desire only that which manifests fulfillment of the desire that satisfies all desiring: Self-realization.

Day 8

*It is necessary for us to understand that
the only Active Principle is Spirit.*
Ernest Holmes

The Action Within Inaction

We must be active not merely for activity's
sake, but for the sake of right action. On the outer
side of life, right action sometimes looks like
inaction.

Since biblical times, there has been a controversy
about action versus inaction. One day, Jesus went to
visit Mary and her sister, Martha. While Mary
chose to sit at the feet of Jesus and learn from him,
Martha remained busy with cleaning the house.
Finally, out of frustration, Martha went to Jesus and
asked, "Lord, do you not care that my sister has left
me to do all the work by myself? Tell her then to
help me." But Jesus answered her, "Martha,
Martha, you are worried and distracted by many
things; there is need of only one thing. Mary has
chosen the better part, which will not be taken away
from her." Mary chose to listen, to expand her consciousness of wisdom and spiritual realization.

There is a level of inactivity where we pull back

from human doing and contemplate a spiritual idea until it is activated within us. What an efficient way to function in life!

Today, meditate until you contact the Presence that thinks through your thoughts, works through your hands, loves through your heart! Know that God, as you, is doing the work that is appointed for you to do. How practical it is to cultivate a rich, inner life with your Spirit! Don't let anyone fool you into thinking that if you do "no-thing" you are living a passive life. Today, don't move until you are moved by the Spirit.

I attune myself to the Activating Principle of the Universe: Pure Spirit. My conscious connection to my Source maintains my balance of action and inaction.

Day 9

Claim Your Divine Dominion!

In the book, *The Agony and the Ecstasy*,
Michelangelo was contemplating David's nature.
What was the most important moment in David's
life? Was it his slingshot practice? Was it the
moment he slew Goliath? No! Michelangelo realized the pivotal moment in David's life was when
he knew in his mind and heart that he *could* slay
Goliath. It was the moment in his heart when the
decision was made, when David turned to the Inner
Authority Principle within his own mind. That
moment changed the course of his destiny!

You are here to wake up to the infinite possibilities of life. Life has already given you all that you
need in your identity as a spiritual being. By waking up to the Real and seeing yourself as you truly
are, you will be in league with the "able-to-do-all-
things" mentality. Then, when the Goliath-size
challenges of life present themselves, you will
know that there is nothing on the outside that is

greater than who and what you are within. Remember, David only had a slingshot and three rocks!

Today, claim your inner dominion as an act of worship. You can accomplish this by first moving into a dynamic, prayerful tryst with the Spirit. Secondly, practice constant gratitude for the blessings in your life; and, thirdly, be a willing instrument of selfless service for the Infinite.

I turn with authority to my own mind and declare that all of God is with me and all of God is for me.

Day 10

Life is ever giving of Itself. We must
receive, utilize and extend the gift.
Success and prosperity are spiritual
attributes belonging to all people.
Ernest Holmes

Living on the Luxurious Lap of Spirit

Are you ready to be wealthy? Do you know what genuine wealth is? Understand that wealth is a state of consciousness, an expanded awareness of having. When you have right understanding of who and what you are, you recognize that you already have all that you need.

I am talking about Universal Law at work here. When we read in Deuteronomy 8:18, "And you shall remember the Lord, your God, for it is He who gives you power to get wealth," understand that the "Lord" means "Law." In using this Law of Life, look also to the first commandment, "Thou shalt not have any other gods before me." When applied to a prosperity teaching, this means not to look to any other source but Spirit for your good. Look nowhere but within to God-consciousness for your good. If you are waiting for the cosmic tumbler to click into place for you to hit the lottery, so you'll get the right job, the right relationship, you are worshiping a false god on the altar of your consciousness.

As you move through the rhythm of your day, don't turn to secondary causative factors for your good! Go directly to First Cause, which is God. When you are attuned to the only Power, Life, Source and Mind that there is, everything works together for your good! Your life will magnify the Lord, and you will live on the lap of Divine Luxury.

The abundance of the Spirit flows in and through me. I am a channel for Its Self-givingness.

Day 11

*Imagination is more important than
knowledge. For knowledge is limited,
whereas imagination embraces the entire
world, stimulating progress, giving birth
to evolution.*
Albert Einstein

Set Your Imagination on Fire

As you begin to hone and refine your imagining
and visioning powers, you will increase your skill
in seeing beyond appearances.

How do you do this? By treating yourself as
you wish others to treat you. Respond to yourself
as you desire the entire Universe to respond to
you! Examine your thoughts and feelings, looking
honestly at what you allow to enter your awareness. What is your inner dialogue with yourself
about yourself? Throughout the day, keep a mental
diary of your inner conversations. Then, at night,
enter them into your journal. Gradually, you will
see a pattern emerge from which you can make any
necessary changes.

Establish a firm intention within yourself.
Declare to yourself with absolute assurance that
your faith is in One Power, One Presence, One
Life. Say this with passion, intensity, power and
depth of feeling. Allow your thoughts, words and

actions to revolve around this conviction. As you deliberately focus on your oneness with Spirit, inviting it to be the Truth in which your consciousness is rooted, your life will change! Your relationship with yourself will transform itself.

Today, begin to live a life filled with the eternal verities of the Spirit, expressing beyond what you can now imagine. You will discover that your imagination is a steppingstone to waking up to what always has been true about you.

My imagination is Spirit's vehicle and It creates mightily through and as me.

Day 12

Uplevel Your Vibratory Contribution!

Some people mentally try to pick up vibrations from things: crystals, good luck charms, candles, pictures, statues, pilgrimages and so on. You are not here merely to catch vibrations *from* things. You are here to imbue things *with* your vibration. Everything in the three-dimensional world is made of Spirit's thought vibrations condensed into the appearance of form. Its vibration of Truth reverberates through you! It radiates outward from you into the world. You are here to anchor the vibration of the Divine in the human dimension.

Wait no longer, submissively hoping and attempting to pick up vibrations from the without. Step out boldly and take possession of your dominion. You will then come into an inner poise, a state of sacred fitness, and this will instantaneously become a component of your vibrational field, of your aura. Then you will overflow with the love energy of God, which will radiate from you as a dynamic force. You will quicken the vibration of God everywhere you go and within everyone you meet.

Today, refuse to see yourself as a recipient of negative vibrations or as a victim of subtle or gross influences around you. Practice broadcasting the high vibrations of the Infinite, remembering that the place upon which you stand is holy simply because *you* are standing there.

My every thought, word and action is a mirror of Spirit's Presence within me. The Divine Idea of Life reflects Itself through me as perfect love, joy, peace and compassion.

Day 13

Your Spiritual Success Story

People have become geniuses at handling failure. Human ingenuity has developed elaborate skills and defense mechanisms for coping with failure. People prepare themselves in advance for failure so they won't be disappointed when things go wrong!

The truth is that you are here to learn how to handle love, joy, creativity and success. You want to develop a structure within that supports an affirmative response to life so that you make yourself receptive to the infinite arenas of success that are all around you.

You accomplish this by conducting a constant re-defining session with yourself, so that moment-by-moment you catch God's definition of who and what you are. It takes courage because it may mean listening to mediocre minds asking, "Who does she think she is?" Never mind! Say to yourself, "This does not move me." Keep your attention on the polestar of God's Infinite Love, cheering you on as you move forward to embrace and embody your spiritual success story.

Today, contemplate the truth that it is God's pleasure to give you the kingdom. Understand that your part is to graciously accept. This moment-by-moment acceptance will ultimately transform any tendencies toward mediocrity. It will create within you a response of strength, confidence and a willingness to more authentically express more of your true nature. Prepare yourself for success!

What I think causes success to unfold in my experience. Divine Love and inspiration flow through me, assuring my success in all my endeavors.

Day 14

*The supreme Awareness, the intimately felt
Presence brings with it a rapture beyond
joy, a knowledge beyond reason, a sensation
more intense than that of life itself.*
Radhakrishnan

Courting the Infinite

There is a longing within you, a mystical ache to express your intrinsic spiritual nature. This inner impulsion lovingly urges you forward until you catch the thought God had at the precise moment It projected you into existence. It is touching to realize that when God thought "You," It thought of nothing else but you. You held Its whole attention, love and awareness.

When through prayer and meditation you awaken your soul's memory of God's original thought of you, you co-create with the Spirit Its unique face appearing as yourself. You are an original work of beauty, light, love, joy and bliss. You have your own personal and intimate relationship with God. It loves you as though you were the only one in the world, because there is only the One. As you consciously cultivate this relationship, as you devotedly court the Divine Presence within you, you are simultaneously cultivating the Original

Expression of Spirit that you are. Conducting this romance with the Infinite satisfies and thrills the soul as nothing else can.

How do you do it? First, you must cultivate a desire for it. Then, just as in any relationship, you invest your love, time and attention. Today, use the little gaps of time to practice the Presence of God. And when you can, spend a longer time in prayer and meditation. The results will astound you.

Today, I consciously commune with the Divine Substance of Love. I am enfolded in Its Presence and consumed by Its Beauty.

*Dreams belong to us. They become for us
the bearers of the new possibility, the
enlarged horizon....giving to our days the
magic of the stars.*
Howard Thurman

On Being Your Own Hero

In my estimation, true heroes and heroines are those who refuse to give up on the part they have been created to play on the stage of life. They go for their dream no matter what obstacles appear in their path. I am saying this to you: Don't give up on your vision!

When you go to bed late at night, or awaken early in the morning when all is yet still in your environment, I know you sometimes sense God's intention for your life. You see through the illusions common to the human experience. The thin veil of unseeing is rent asunder and you see God's idea for your life. It is then that you no longer cling to the conspiracy of human definitions that seek to convince you to give up, to believe there is not enough good to go around. You rise above all this and realize that you are surrounded by spiritual ideas. There comes a breakthrough, a recognition of the blueprint of excellence which is the Real

Self! Then the prophets of doom and gloom take up no space in your mental household. You become a glorious agent of transformation in your own life and in the lives of others.

Today, continue to nourish your dreams. Hold fast to your vision and do something every day to bring it into manifestation. Everything is possible in God because God is the Infinite Possibility within everything. Know that you are God's beloved in whom God is well pleased. Never give up on yourself!

Awake in the Cosmic Dream, I fashion my life according to Spirit's perfect vision of me as Its individualized expression.

Day 16

...Enter into his court with praise.
Holy Bible

The Praise-Phrase of the Heart

When you develop favorite praise-phrases of your own, you catch the realization that there is power in praise. When you become wedded to a phrase of absolute spiritual truth that reverberates in the heart, mind and soul of you, the vibration of that phrase transforms your life. You begin to see the world through this praise-phrase.

Why is that? Because the only malady you suffer from is the illusion of being separate from the Spirit, separate from God. All problems have their genesis in that great delusion. When repeated with sincerity, devotion and explicit faith, your praise-phrase drowns out anything unlike itself. It drowns out the cry of the world of appearances that tells you that what you see with the five senses alone is real.

What most people call thinking is for the most part recycled opinion! It's really not thinking at all. Rather, it is repeated statements of density and grossness lodged in the collective thinking, the popular opinion of the day.

All of your experiences are the result of your own self-contemplation. So when you talk to your Self and not to the world, when you listen to your Self and not to the voice of the world, you will hear the still, small voice leading, guiding and comforting you, making all the crooked places straight. Consistent use of your praise-phrase causes you to expand your awareness and see the way God sees the world and your part in it.

Today, look at your life experiences and invite a potent praise-phrase to speak itself within you. Write it down, say it to yourself and say it out loud until it sets your heart on fire.

I perceive the face of Spirit throughout my environment and I give praise to That which reveals to me my own Divinity.

*The gnostic being's actions in the world
will be enlightened by a sense of the Divine
Reality. This enables him to take
all of life into himself while still
remaining the spiritual Self.*
Sri Aurobindo

Access Your Accessibility

As I was driving on the freeway, my Inner Voice said, "You have access to the human dimension." In an flash of intuition, I understood the beauty and subtlety of these words. It's like this: You have access to your car, but you are not your car. You have access to your house, but you are not your house. You have access to a loving human relationship, but neither participant is the relationship. In other words, each one of us has access to the human dimension but that does not mean we are merely human.

You are not merely a human being who has limited access to the spiritual dimension. No! You are a Divine Being who has been given access to the playing field of human experience. This is the essence of gnosticism, a body of spiritual knowledge imbedded in the New Thought-Ancient Wisdom teaching.

You have been born into the three-dimensional

world to access the Divine Presence hiding behind a creation that seems so solid. You didn't do anything to earn this experience; it is yours simply because of who you are as a Divine Emanation of the Spirit. Now is the time, where you are is the place, and who you are is deserving. As you seek to access the Divine Dimension present right where you are, you will manifest a high degree of freedom which comes from realizing that you have access to the Promised Land of infinite possibilities.

This day, consciously access the Divine. Go below the surface to the truth being offered to you in every experience. Your access code is *I Am.*

I realize, feel, hear and see the Divine in all forms of inner and outer life. I freely access the Divine Presence and joyously commune with It on the altar of my own being.

Day 18

There Are No Loopholes in Spiritual Law

Where you put your attention, there is your power. Why? Because where you place your attention you invest your energy, and energy empowers your life. The words you speak are filled with your energy. The truth contained in your words determines their vibratory potency. To the degree that you attune yourself to the vibratory frequencies of love, compassion, truth, discernment and honesty, a vibration will go forth from you that contributes to the upliftment of your own consciousness and the collective consciousness.

You cannot fool Spiritual Law! It produces effects in exact correspondence to what is held in your consciousness. No matter in what manner of sweet or commanding tones you think or speak your words, the Law instantly responds to the consciousness behind them. All language is sound vibration. The Law responds not to your literal words, but to their vibratory qualities.

Be aware that even the people around you respond to your energy, which is the vibration you release from your mental atmosphere. Examine the purity of your motive for expressing. Pause and ask yourself, "What is the vibratory content of this emotion? What is my motive for making this particular statement, performing this act? Will it uplift, clarify? Is it necessary, kind, true?"

Today, be wise in investing your energy. By doing so, you will reap a high yield from your spiritual bank account. The dividends will be awesome!

I know that the Law of Life placed only one Divine Verdict upon me: That I am Its beloved expression, perfectly fulfilling my destiny in accordance with Its perfect Law.

Day 19

*The real Self is God-given and cannot be
denied. Individuality means self-choice,
volition, complete freedom.*
Ernest Holmes

Live from Your First Nature

You, like all people, represent a composite idea
of the Godhead and Its qualities of Divine Love,
Wholeness, Divine Right Action and Divine
Intelligence. All of this is within you, but it must
be activated. Once activated, it must be consciously
exercised until it becomes second nature to you.

Your first nature is Spirit. But at times you have
allowed your second nature–your habits and false
beliefs–to take precedence over your first nature.
When thoughts of lack, limitation, doubt and fear
are lodged in the subjective mind, a groove is
forged and a habit is created. These habits begin to
dictate your experience. Spiritual Mind Treatment
regrooves those hard-held places in consciousness
where mental habits have taken up residence.
Through daily practice of affirmative prayer, you
direct your conscious mind to impress your
subjective mind with thoughts of positivity, with
words of truth of who and what you already

are: a spiritual being completely free from undesirable habits. A new order of mental and emotional response is set into motion. Experiment with this, make it your own.

Today, refuse to play by the dictates of personal "bad" or "good" history. Play as a free spirit who is bound only by the habit of love for the Infinite. Don't miss your prayer and meditation time. Use it to immerse yourself in the qualities of the Spirit. You will then demonstrate that the Spirit has no limitations in Its expression as you. The Love that you are knows no boundaries; the Life that you are knows no boundaries. As you learn to go deep in prayer, your first nature and your second nature will come into harmony and balance. Seeming miracles will take place. Go forth and multiply the consciousness of miracles. I know you can!

I recognize and appreciate the God-Self dwelling within me. I give this Divine Presence that is my life the freedom to be Itself in and as me.

In the arrangement of the world there is
seen the expression of delight, which
shows that in the Universe, over and above
the meaning of matter and form, there
is a message conveyed through the
magic touch of individual personality.
Rabindranath Tagore

Delight as the Light

You are literally the delight of God. In a moment of pure intention, supported by your sincerity of practice, you will hear your brother Jesus saying, "You are the light, the light that lights up every man and woman who comes into the world." It is because Spirit yearns to share Itself with you that It placed Its Essence within you. This Divine Presence within your soul consciousness is what allows you to commune with God. Don't keep the Spirit waiting! Doing so postpones your delight in experiencing a relationship of unimaginable beauty. Prayer and meditation are the divine doorways through which you walk into communion with the Delight of all life.

When you set your intention to move through this incarnation celebrating as the Light that you are, you will be lifted out of the secondary causative factors of life, which may have hypnotized you into believing that you are here on earth to cope with your existence through the overcoming of problems and challenges. Wake up to the realization that, as Sri Aurobindo put it, "To seek for Delight is the fundamental impulse of Life; to find, possess and fulfill It is Life's whole motive." God-adoring hearts beat to the rhythm of Cosmic Love, Cosmic Delight.

Today, be one of the greatest lovers God has ever known. With every step you take, talk to God about the delight you experience in the realization of your oneness with pure Spirit. With every breath, realize you glow with God. Then you will know absolutely that the flame of the Godhead is always alight within you. You will realize that Spirit's delight is in your seeking of Itself within yourself. Once this discovery is made, Cosmic Delight engulfs in oneness the seeker, the act of seeking, and That which is sought.

The Spirit ever gives of Itself in lavish abundance.
I receive the gift and delight in its sweetness.

Day 21

So, when this corruptible shall have put on incorruption, and this mortal shall have put on immortality, then shall be brought to pass the saying that is written, Death is swallowed up in victory. O death, where is thy sting? O grave, where is thy victory?
Holy Bible

Birthless, Deathless Eternality!

What I realize so clearly is that we are not born, nor do we die. Absolutely not! The truth is we appear and disappear. As the *Bhagavad Gita* says, "N'er the Spirit was born, n'er shall it die." In truth, you are a birthless, deathless being who has the privilege to appear and disappear on the planet, always to reveal more and never less than your true Self. You are not phenomena, you are nomena, which is another way of saying that you are not an illusory appearance. You are a thought creation of the Spirit.

As you peer below the surface of the human landscape, you will see that individuals build their lives on one fundamental fear: annihilation of the individual self. If you build your life on the fear of death or loss of that which you hold dear, then all of your efforts are aimed at avoiding the inevitable loss of the human body. The body is temporal; *you are eternal!* You can eradicate the fear of death from your life through understanding and accepting that you are an immortal being. Your soul already knows this. Build your life on faith, not fear. Be receptive to the truth that you are inseparable from Life itself, that your existence as an individualized expression of the Spirit cannot die, for that which is of the Spirit knows only unlimited Life.

Today, during your time of meditation and prayer, contact the innate Changelessness within you. Identify yourself with the soul, not with matter. To the degree that your attention is stayed on the Real through affirmative prayer and meditation, the Real and Eternal takes charge of your life. Today, see if there are areas into which you have not invited the Infinite to illumine your understanding of your true nature. Extend the invitation now, and see how bliss, joy, fearlessness and unbroken communion with God take over your life.

Today I celebrate the Eternal Spirit at the center of my being. I set my eyes on the Living Light of God and am established in heaven consciousness.

Day 22

By supreme devotion my own realize Me and
My nature – what and who I am;
after knowing these truths, they
quickly make entry into Me.
Bhagavad Gita

An evolved soul is always a worshipper of God.
Ernest Holmes

Whole-Souled Devotion

Today, call forth the whole-souled devotion of your heart. Unleash it in your life! Live in the great mystery, in that sense of awe at the Infinite Possibilities that are right within you and all around you. Metaphorically fall on your knees at how healings happen, how insights and breakthroughs occur, how creativity expresses through you, how Grace moves through you, compelling you to intuitively do the right thing at the right time.

Be aware that when the scripture tells you to fear the Lord, it is saying to stand humbly before the magnificence, order and unconditional love of the Universe. Whole-souled devotion generates a purity that requalifies every thought form, directing your subjective thinking toward seeing the Face of God in every experience, walking through the feet of all humanity, smiling at you from within all creation. Devotion will do this for you.

You may think this is an impractical way to live, that it is more available to monks and yogis. Or, perhaps you see yourself as not inclined to mystical experiences. Such thinking is merely the hypnotism of the race suggestion into which you have been lulled by living too much on the surface of your consciousness. Contemplate the truth that not even your greatest human lover can give you the eternal love of God. They did not create you; God did. You came into this world alone and you will leave it alone, except for the Eternal Lover Who leaves you never. Does this not make it worthwhile to cultivate an intimate and personal relationship with the One who is the Author of Love itself?

Contemplate the Eternality of the Spirit's love for you and it will transform every misery into a steppingstone to joy. God, God, God! You are God's hands and feet, serving Itself in all of Its human selves through you, loving Itself in all through your own heart. Can you imagine a life for yourself devoted to anything but the One who loves you so much It thought you forth into existence? Wake up today and cultivate whole-souled devotion for the All-encompassing Presence.

I surrender to the all-consuming Love of the Spirit. I am absorbed by this Divine Presence, so personal that it has personalized Itself as myself.

Day 23

Give away all that thou hast and follow me.
Jesus the Christ

Reflections on Surrender

It was Saint Augustine who spoke about people who go to God only half way. He was describing individuals who are willing to give up *some* of their time for prayer and meditation, *some* of their negative thought patterns and habits. However, they don't trust quite enough to go all the way with God. They keep one eye on God, and one eye on the external world as their source of fulfillment, accepting that which can be known with a false certitude by the five senses.

When you send out a real soul-call to God, Infinite Omniscience responds. A vibration is sent from you into the Universe, which draws into your experience that which will support the fulfillment of your desire. Your humility in asking for Divine assistance places you in a receptive position as you surrender your human understanding to Divine Wisdom.

When both eyes are placed on God, you have your ticket to transformation. You buy it with the spiritual coin of wisdom, humility, faith and detachment.

Today, give up false mental attachments and beliefs! Free yourself from the delusion that anything external can fulfill the hunger of your soul for God-consciousness. Follow the Christ Presence within and you will liberate your consciousness from all that is unlike your true Self. As you passionately devote yourself to knowing God, you will be able to override the demands of the little ego and faithfully surrender to the One who is the finisher of your faith.

Today's practice is for you to let go and let God.

I joyfully release all vestiges of false belief and surrender my whole attention to the overshadowing Presence of Truth within me. Conscious communion with Spirit is my way of life.

Day 24

All around us there are these surprises of
kindly interference, manifesting the grace of
life, the tenderness and mercy of God. Thus
our hearts are wooed into thanksgiving and
praise for what has been given to us.
Howard Thurman

The Alchemy of Gratitude

Gratitude is where freedom and destiny meet, because gratitude is a divine doorway to the fulfillment of destiny. When you consciously choose to express thanksgiving, this sets causation into motion to manifest your destiny of Wholeness in every expression of your life.

Gratitude generates enthusiasm, the fuel on the spiritual path that propels us Godward. "Enthusiasm" comes from the Greek, "theos," which means "to be in God." Today, enthusiastically leap into gratitude for no other reason than that you are alive to celebrate your existence as an emanation of God!

Remember, however, that you cannot misuse gratitude, thinking that if you master this quality you can manipulate Universal Law to fulfill your desires. You cannot manipulate yourself into the good life by being grateful. That is the talk of the surface mind. Gratitude becomes causation for greater demonstrations of good in your life when you sincerely express thankfulness for your existence as an individualized expression of God.

True gratitude is a way of life. Begin today. When you wake up in the morning, let your first thought be one of thanksgiving that you have another day to walk in the love of God. As you go through your day, see the Giver behind all of the gifts freely being given to you.

As events present themselves in your experience, train your consciousness to be in gratitude independent of judging them as desirable or undesirable. Remain detached. Then at night, train your last thought before sleep to be one of thanksgiving for the miracle of knowing God, whose pleasure it is to give you the kingdom.

Today I fling open wide the door of my gratitude in humble recognition of the Divine Presence that holds me in the Eternal Embrace of its Self-Givingness.

Day 25

*Your love has made me sure. I am ready to
forsake this worldly life and surrender to
the magnificence of Your Being.*
Rumi

It's an Inside Job!

The awareness you crave is a function of the inner life. It can never be realized through circumstances, relationships or accomplishments. In other words, you cannot find true satisfaction outside of fulfilling your highest destiny: realization of your oneness with God.

I want you to wake up today! If you believe that you will be complete after you find the right relationship, the better job, a bigger house, that hotter investment, the accomplishment of a particular goal, you are asleep in the human dream of *maya*, which is the sleep of human delusion. Any such fulfillment is only temporary. The quest of looking for wholeness outside of yourself is not the way it works. It's an inside job!

Failure to recognize the true nature of your life's quest creates a syndrome of identity crisis. It will continue until you turn within to the only true Source of fulfillment and develop an active relationship with this Supreme Reality. Begin now to cultivate your spiritual sensitivity to this Presence. Talk to Spirit in the language of your heart and notice how sweetly and eagerly It responds to you.

Today, know that the Spirit delights in bestowing heavenly treasures upon you. A magnificent awakening awaits your willingness to receive them. If you are callous to the truth that Spirit "stands at the door and knocks," how shall It come into your experience? Cultivate sensing and knowing that Spirit longs to give fully of Itself to you. Live, move and have your awareness in this reality and you will come to understand what Jesus meant when he said, "It is the Father's good pleasure to give you the kingdom." The door of receptivity opens from the inside. Today, swing it wide open and expect a blessing that will fill your heart to overflowing.

I sense the Divine Presence at the center of my being. My mind, heart and soul drink deeply from this Divine Well and forever quench my thirst.

Day 26

*When with deliberate intent I have turned
my back on truth and peace, Thou hast
searched for and found me. I cannot escape
Thy Scrutiny! I would not escape Thy
Love!*
Howard Thurman

Peace: Habitat of the Spirit

Peace is a quality of the Spirit that is everywhere present. Peace as a dynamic harmony is what you are called to reveal first within your own consciousness, and then in your world. Thoughts and actions born of the inner peace of your soul are in alignment with the Laws of the Universe.

All of the peace that you could ever desire is already within you. It saturates the Universe and everything in it. You contact this peace through prayer and meditation. At first, your meditative silence may seem empty, punctuated by interludes of distracting thoughts. Continue to sit until the silence is transmuted into stillness. If you persevere, you will be lifted into a state of rapture that transcends the human realm. Even now it is calling unto you. Its voice remains subtle until you attune yourself to Its transcendent vibration.

The Spirit is so humble It will not force Itself into your awareness. But what great joy It knows when you willingly enter the temple of bliss within your own soul.

Throughout this day, stop frequently to breathe and touch that place within you that is the "peace that surpasseth all understanding." Let it be carried on the wings of your thoughts, words and actions. Through calmness, keep your mental and nervous systems relaxed so that they may catch the intuitive guidance whispered to you by Spirit. Peace is another way of practicing the Presence of God.

Like a river, Spirit's peace flows through my being, soothing, warming and harmonizing my body, mind and soul.

*We are all immersed in the atmosphere of
our own thinking. This decides what shall
take place in our lives.*
Ernest Holmes

Thinker, Thinking, Thought

Thought is energy. The quality of your thought is reflected through your emotions, speech and behavior. The thoughts that pass through your awareness translate themselves into your experiences. That which you think reality to be is your experience.

In the Bible we read, "Hear this, O people, who have eyes, but do not see, who have ears, but do not hear." The metaphysical interpretation of this passage is that until you are fully awakened, you cannot directly perceive Reality, nor does it outpicture as the experience of your life. Instead, your understanding is processed through the limitations of your thinking about Reality, which then becomes the body of your affairs.

The survival level of mentality is reactive, unthinking. It is based on a mistaken mind-set from judgments based on input from the five senses and limitations of an unenlightened consciousness.

Through prayer and meditation, determine to shake off the dust of spiritual ignorance and free yourself from wrong thinking. As you commingle the self with the Self, your thoughts reveal the thinking of the Divine Mind that is within you. You move from thinking and analyzing to direct, intuitive perception of the Truth. Prayer facilitates your awareness of the Self; meditation expands your consciousness to merge with the Self. As the little self recedes and you touch Reality, thought becomes requalified, purified and aligned with the Original Thinker.

Today, begin to cultivate a hunger to live life at this level.

My whole consciousness is alive with the inspired thoughts of God. I am impregnated with Divine Ideas. I think directly from Spirit and let Divine Intelligence have Its way with me.

*At the height of laughter, the Universe
is flung into a kaleidoscope
of new possibilities.*
Jean Houston

Laugh the Laugh of Buddha

As you mature spiritually, your natural gifts of the
soul rise to the surface and express through personality, which is your Divine Individuality. This
allows you to appreciate your Divinity, including
the quirks that are uniquely your own way of moving
in the world. You develop the ability to not take
yourself so seriously, to laugh at yourself. Then
energy is freed up, the endorphins rush and the life
force harmoniously flows through you. The ego
loses its tight grip on your concerns about how others
see you, how the world is totaling up its evaluation
of you.

Your readiness and willingness to laugh at yourself creates a gap through which you may see yourself more clearly. The reactive mind slows down,
and there is a perception of clarity. More of life,
love and joy can then move through you.

I love the image of the laughing Buddha.
Looking at or visualizing it causes a welling up

of joy in my mind. Buddha-mind sees clearly through the appearance of humanity's hypnotic ignorance to the clear Light of Truth that all is well with our souls. It sees what sociologist Peter L. Berger described when saying, "The final illusion is power, while laughter is the final truth."

Today, know with me that humor is a gateway to wisdom. Walk through it and you will master a spiritual skill that will create space between you and the fictional character you call yourself. It will put the smile of Buddha that is in your soul upon your face.

The Cosmic Laughter of Spirit bathes my soul in joy. I see with clear seeing and all that I do is from the pure joy of being.

Day 29

*The goal of life is God! The source of life is
God! God is the goal of man's life,
the end of all his seeking,
the meaning of all his striving.*
Howard Thurman

The Soul Aflame

Throughout this day, be courageous enough to not turn on your television or to participate in any outer distractions until you make contact with your soul. Be willing to say, "I'm not moving from this place until Divine Contact is made." When Buddha sat under the banyan tree, he refused to move until the mysteries of the Universe were revealed to him.

The Christian mystic Meister Eckhart said, "The eyes with which I see God are the eyes through which God sees me." When you set your intention to be serious about your God-Self, your God-Self will be serious about you. Mystical secrets will reveal themselves to you. What are those secrets? That you are now, always have been and ever shall be one with God.

Brother Lawrence, a humble monk, lived in the world as if only he and God existed. He performed every activity in the conscious company of Spirit.

There was no separation between his prayer time, meditation time and time of service. It was all one worshipful action of Divine Love. Living in this state of consciousness is the purpose of existence.

You see, when you make time for your soul to be enthralled with the Divine Presence, you are raised up to divine heights of oneness with the Spirit. But this doesn't come simply by saying or affirming it is so. No! You must be willing to give the Spirit more than a small percentage of your time.

Today, determine to practice spiritual discipline, which means consciously setting aside time to cultivate your relationship with the Spirit. Once you form this habit, I guarantee you won't want to miss your Divine Appointment with the Infinite.

God is first in my life. The beginning, middle and end is God. I live, move and have my being in the light of this recognition.

> *Your very life-breath must become the conscious, timeless affirmation of Reality by Reality, "I am It, It is I."*
> Ramakrishna Paramahansa

Eden Consciousness

It is wonderful to realize that we live in a Universe that offers us a continuum of transformational experiences. It is always working on Its own behalf for greater expression of what It is. And It places before you the same mandate in the form of an inner calling from the soul to fulfill yourself by doing in the microcosm what the Universe does in the macrocosm: evolve into ever greater expression.

What does this mean? It means that you step into your Eden consciousness. A day will come when you take a breath and see through your own disguise. You will see that you are the Life of God fulfilling Itself. Then, Eden consciousness–in which you have existed since the beginning of time–overtakes you. Your prayer becomes, "I am what Thou art; Thou art what I am." This recognition will free you from the shackles of ignorance which cause a false belief in lack, limitation, fear, doubt and worry. It will allow you to stand unshaken amidst circumstances and say with the Psalmist, "I lift up my hands and call on your name. My soul is satisfied as with a rich feast, and my mouth praises you with joyful lips. When I think of you on my bed and meditate on you in the watches of the night…in the shadow of your wings I sing for joy. My soul clings to you."

Today, consciously incline your inner ear and listen to the call of your heart. Listen and say "yes." More good than you can imagine is in store for those who give up the little sense of self for the Self.

Divine Presence ever whispers Its name to me. My name is written on the palm of Its hand: I AM that I am.

Day 31

Truth is the flight of the alone to the Alone.
Plotinus

Spiritual Loyalty

Wouldn't it just be a mess if the Spirit placed your answer in someone else? Spiritual loyalty is looking within to the Self for Divine guidance and following Its direction to the next step in the soul's unique pattern of unfoldment.

Some teachers demand unconditional loyalty. But who and what you are is too big to be confined to one method of spiritual awakening. There really is no such thing as spiritual promiscuity.

Different dimensions of our consciousness may require a specific teacher and teaching for expansion and growth. For example, if you integrate one path of prayer with yet a different path of meditation, and another teaching's technique for practicing the Presence of God, that is good! Even if the Spirit directs you to take a sabbatical from your routine of practices and to simply remain still, it is good. It is all good.

To grow up spiritually means to take personal responsibility for your growth and development. You drop followership for leadership by Spirit. While you learn from your teachers, you don't make them your gods. You don't pedestalize them, thinking they will do the work for you, that their mere words transform you, that they take on your karma and relieve you of your individual responsibility to do the inner work required for you to wake up.

You may have many teachers, but only one Master: God alone. You must follow your own unique pattern of unfoldment directed from within.

Today, approach your spiritual path as though for the first time. Ask the Spirit to guide you. Remember, spiritual paths are merely the maps, the road guides to awakening. Once there, you may throw away the maps.

My mind is centered in heaven and I respond to the leadership of the Spirit. No intermediary stands between the Spirit and my soul. God in me is the one true Source of my fulfillment and awakening.

Day 32

Love is the victor in every case. Love breaks down the iron bars of thought, shatters the walls of material belief, severs the chain of bondage which thought has imposed, and sets the captive free.
Ernest Holmes

Stop Living Life on the Layaway Plan!

Do you have a material concept of good? If so, you will never be content, for there is never enough of that which doesn't satisfy. Speaking to his disciples about the hypnotic nature of material desire, a spiritual master once cautioned, "Ever fed, never satisfied."

The Good of God is Intangible Substance. When you ask in faith believing, this Substance takes the form of all things necessary for the fulfillment of your life's purpose, including the tangible prosperity you require. Your part is to access the divine dimension of your being which allows you to simply give in and let Divine Love be a constant current flowing through and as your life. Willingly enter into the stream of Love and watch how you are carried by the unstoppable dynamic of God's Love calling you to be bigger than you ever thought you could be.

Take all the stops out! Stop living your life on

the layaway plan, reserving some of life today to live for tomorrow. Use the spiritual coin of surrender and take your life off the layaway plan!

All the love your heart can hold, all the success you are meant to experience is already within you, begging to be released through your love energy. Today, open the floodgates of your heart and pour out a blessing of Love into your own life. Then see how outrageously rich you are in the gifts of the Spirit.

Today my every thought, word and action is permeated with Divine Love. Love takes me over as I surrender to the Divine Presence, living as the Self of all.

Day 33

*You have a silent partnership with the Infinite.
Rest in this divine assurance and this divine
security. This is more than a sentiment. Know
that the Spirit flows in transcendent loveliness
into your world of thought and form, that It
flows through your whole being, spiritual,
emotional, mental and physical.*
Ernest Holmes

Fuel for the Soul

I want you to be aware that at whatever level of
consciousness you live, you use a particular type of
mental fuel to propel yourself into mental, emotional, psychological and spiritual activity.

The kind of fuel you burn goes out from you as
a vibration impacting your individual world and the
collective consciousness of our planet. The ecolog-
ical structure and the sociological structure of the
world are a reflection of the collective consciousness, the collective agreement about what reality is.

When you are pulled into an awareness of who
and what you really are, you melt away any seeming
boundaries between you and your true nature as an
individualized expression of God. Your fuel
changes and you begin to live on the pure energy of
Spirit. You no longer pollute your consciousness
with negativity, lack or limitation. Fill up your consciousness with the highest octane available

and energize your inner and outer world with your realization of oneness, of wholeness.

Spiritual seers, fueled by Divine Love and attunement with the Laws of the Universe, remain ever aligned to the Will of God. By "Will of God" I mean the unique pattern of unfoldment designed for each individual soul, one's dharma, the Buddhist word for "right purpose." As you activate your interest in your dharma, you automatically develop an interest in the presence of God.

Today, watch how through an inner loyalty to your dharma you become so highly charged with Divine Love that everywhere you go, with whomsoever you meet, you exude the fragrance of this love, filling your words and deeds with compassion and loving kindness.

I wed myself to Divine Love and bestow its essence upon everything. My every motive, thought and action is fueled by the energy of my commitment and love for my spiritual journey.

> *The highest expression of gratitude is the*
> *realization that God is the invisible source*
> *of all that is visible, and that He is respon-*
> *sible for all of the good on this earth and on*
> *all the planets.*
> Joel Goldsmith

The Yoga of Gratitude

Today, I invite you to begin developing a consistent practice of what I call the Yoga of Gratitude. When you think of yoga, commonly what comes to mind are the various yoga *asanas*, or postures. The Yoga of Gratitude is very much like a yogic stretch. When the body is protracted into an unfamiliar posture, it releases tension, toxins and energy. Similarly, as life's experiences stretch your self-awareness, the surface mind releases toxins of the ego's resistance.

Over the years, the mind has adopted certain coping and defense mechanisms which were necessary at the time to protect you from what appeared to be the uncertainties of life. Or, perhaps you were afraid to be grateful for fear that you were telling the Universe you liked a particular experience exactly the way it was. As you develop the inner discipline of gratitude, you will not only realize that it is a natural quality of your soul, you will also notice more and more things for which to be grateful. Your consciousness will come to trust this mental posture and will no longer release egoic toxins.

By taking the mental posture of being equally grateful for the blessings and the challenges in your life, spiritual maturity occurs. The more you include unconditional gratitude in your spiritual practice, the line blurs between blessings and challenges; they are understood to be gifts of the Spirit, equal in value to your spiritual progress. The Yoga of Gratitude stretches your capacity to assume this humble and receptive pose.

Today, luxuriate yourself with several long, slow yogic breaths; let go and surrender into gracious gratitude. Breathe again, and step out of time and space into the Eternal Moment of Now. Breathe again, and step into Self-realization. This Cosmic Breath is breathed into you from God. Be grateful.

Life is the Spirit's gift to me. I enter fully into the Blessed Incarnation that is my very Self. I walk in the light of thanksgiving consciousness, bestowing my blessing upon all whom I see, all that I think, say and do.

Day 35

Sacred Site, Holy Site

Since the beginning of time, the heart of the New Thought-Ancient Wisdom mystical teaching has revealed that you and I are the sacred site of God. When you solidly embody the realization that, "Ye are the temple of the Living God," you cause the transcendental, transformative, Infinite Presence to so powerfully move within and as you that any seeming contradiction to this truth is forever removed from your consciousness.

Don't wait for whatever future circumstances you think represent the ideal conditions for your spiritual enlightenment. Oh no! Take the highest vision of Christ Consciousness that you can hold and present its Reality to your consciousness right now. In this instant, allow for the holy site of the Infinite to be your inward sight. Then no longer will you be under the karmic influence of human law; rather, you will be governed by Grace. Then you will begin to fluently articulate the vision of your life in accordance with Spirit's idea of Its expression as you. In that instant, the love, purity, joy, wisdom, harmony, beauty and ecstasy of the Universe will be revealed to you by the Presence of Love Itself.

Today, withdraw from living in some future fantasy and live right now as if the entire Universe is conspiring on your behalf, because it is. Carry yourself as if all your needs are met, because it has been so since the beginning of time.

Today I walk in the Spirit's Presence, quickened by the realization of my Awakened Self. Everything that I think, say and do is touched by this Divine Awareness.

Day 36

What truth do you know, and how
steadfast are you in its application?
Joel Goldsmith

The Masquerade Is Over!

There is that part of yourself that exists outside of the relativity of time and space, ever aware of your true identity. This Reality is always presenting itself into your inner awareness. The question is: Are you sensitive enough to recognize it? Compared to the outward expression of life experienced through the five senses, the Spirit's movement within your consciousness is subtle, detectable through the inner quietude found in deep meditation. Once you have sufficiently tasted of this soul-nectar, the Spirit found in the stillness reveals Itself in the activity of your exterior life. This is how the mystics live. Whether they are engaged in inward or outward activity, they remain ever aware, ever awake, ever worshipful at the Feet of Omnipresence.

Your practice of affirmative prayer and meditation penetrates the subjective region of consciousness, stripping away the mask of your acceptance of the illusions of lack, limitation, rationalization and materialism. A revolution of values takes place within you and the masquerade is over! You no longer hide behind the ramparts of your insecurities and uncertainties. Instead, you stand victorious in your inner dominion because affirmative prayer and meditation have anchored you in your true identity as a spiritual being.

You are both the producer and actor on the stage of your life. Keep your consciousness on the Spirit as Director, and you will come into the awareness that all of the props you need to support your life have already been provided. If you imagine that something is missing, it is because you haven't caught your cue to look deeply enough within and find there the Source and Substance of your supply.

This truth is the supreme spiritual idea held in the mind of God about you as an individualized expression of Itself, imbued with Its qualities: bliss, love, joy, wisdom, harmony, balance, affluence, beauty, peace and order. Stand in ownership of this state of consciousness right now, powerfully claiming your divine inheritance. Today, walk in the world as if nothing is missing.

I consecrate myself to the purpose of my being. I dedicate my thoughts, words and actions to the Spirit, and am a clear, pure channel of Its expression.

> *Love the Lord thy God with all thy heart,*
> *with all thy mind and with all thy*
> *strength.*
> Holy Bible

The Eternal Lover

All of your spiritual work is a quest for your true identity. But the Self cannot be fooled! It will never be enough to merely parrot the truth, "God is all that there is; all that I am is God."

Belief and realization are not synonymous. When you plummet to the depths of your soul in meditation and prayer, transporting yourself beyond the surface appearance world of the five senses, you taste the honey of God-realization. You drink the nectar poured into the soul by the Infinite. Belief is transmuted into realization as individual consciousness merges in ecstatic oneness with the Eternal Lover of the cosmos.

That, for me, is it! I invite you to join me in choosing to live in this consciousness. The fact is that you have no other choice because eventually you must wake up! Of course, there is a certain level of discipline involved. Even though the Lover of the Universe is patient, you cannot expect

It to respond to lukewarm advances! You have to mean business with God by honoring your divine tryst to pray and meditate on a daily basis and to practice the Presence of God in the little gaps of time throughout the day.

Beloved, I do not say these words to induce guilt; I speak to you in this way because I know what you have to look forward to. I don't want your divine fulfillment to be postponed one moment longer! Once you have tasted it, no longer will you see yourself simply as a separate individual participating in your relationships and the affairs of your life. Rather, you will know yourself as an emanation of God, swimming with all creation in an ocean of oneness.

Today, lean your whole heart into your desire for a personal and intimate oneness with the Spirit. If you do so, you will discover that the Infinite Presence hungers also for your love and attention.

I know, and know that I know, that the unconditional Divine Love of the Spirit is the incomparable Grace of my life.

> *Let your light so shine before men, that*
> *they may see your good works, and glorify*
> *your Father which is in heaven.*
> Holy Bible

Develop Your Spiritual Faculties

When Nicodemus asked Jesus to describe an individual who lives by spiritual values, Jesus indicated that such a person is born of the Spirit. He then spoke metaphorically, saying that to discern whether an individual has indeed been born again, it is rather like trying to see the wind: You can feel and hear the wind, but you cannot see its origin through the five senses. The reason is because *that which is spiritual can only be discerned by that which is spiritual.* It is rather like the familiar cliché, "It takes one to know one."

Approach Jesus' statement as you would a Buddhist koan, which is a contemplative question that cannot be solved by the rational mind. Quiet yourself and intuit this: "What spiritual faculties would I have to develop to discern that which is spiritual?" As you meditate and pray, dive below the surface of your three-dimensional being into your non-dimensional Self, to the intuitive consciousness where there is direct perception of Truth. As you arrive at that place of alignment with the Love and Law of the Universe, spiritual awareness will permeate your consciousness. You have traded in reliance on your natural human resources for reliance on the Spirit alone.

Contemplate what spiritual discernment means and how you may apply it to all areas of your life. Embody this quality in your consciousness and you will revolutionize the experience known as your life.

Today I practice divine discernment. As I lift my soul unto the Spirit, the winds of its glory cause me to behold the Eternal and reveal Its Presence in my thoughts, words and actions.

Day 39

No more words. Hear only the voice within.
Rumi

Living by Soul-Force

The more you live your life from a deep connection with the Spirit, the more you will experience and express your Soul-Force.

When Jesus said, "Blessed are the meek, for they shall inherit the earth," he was laying out an efficient blueprint for living and moving in the world. When you are meek, you are humble. When you are humble, you are in tune with your Soul-Force, you remain strong and secure in the Spirit. The need to pump up the false ego built by the surface mind simply falls away. You will then be free from running your rackets of defense mechanisms, pretense and fears that convince the little ego you will be annihilated if you don't heed its voice, if you don't cling to your personal history.

When with humility and sincerity you say "yes" to the still small voice speaking within, your Soul-Force takes over, and you step into your authentic identity as an individualized expression of of the Living Spirit.

Today, ignite your Soul-Force by accepting that you are just as significant as the greatest saint who ever lived and was loved by the Spirit. Hear Its voice echoing within your heart, "You are my beloved in whom I am well pleased."

I offer myself as a humble instrument of the Spirit. I allow my Soul-Force to express in Its fullest form and all is well with my soul.

The rhythm of my heart is the birth and death of all that are alive.
Thich Nhat Hanh

A Revolution of Values

Do you know that a "Revolution of Values" is now taking place? Slowly but surely, the collective mind is responding to a spiritual implosion occurring on our planet. This revolution is drawing humanity into a global agreement that is providing an avenue for the Kingdom of God to reveal Itself on earth as peace, love, harmony, order and balance.

Any "Revolution of Values" is birthed first through the expansion of one's own heart. An initial indication that you are entering this expanded state is that you feel an altruistic urge to get involved in serving others. However, there remains a lingering sense of a separate self wanting to be known as a do-gooder, to receive recognition for being a philanthropist. As you mature out of this stage, you will come to a great discovery: There is no "other" to serve! When you serve "other," you are actually serving yourself, because every person is an individualized expression of the only Life that there is: God!

There is only One Power and One Presence everywhere present. When you consciously align yourself with the One Life that is humbly and joyously running the Universe, you then realize that you are never walking alone, that you are never serving alone. You are moving through your life in league with the Infinite. Cosmic awareness kicks in and you move through society as an agent of transformation in the "Revolution of Values."

Today, consciously set the intention to offer yourself to the Spirit as a willing conduit for the love, peace, joy, wisdom and harmony of the Universe to flow through you, touching your entire environment. As you do, there will be a revolution within your soul. Do not be surprised to find yourself making use of your free time differently, your money differently, your talents differently, and your mind and heart differently.

Today, my heart tenderly embraces all creation as my very own. I open myself and allow the Universe to flow through me as Its very Self.

About the Author

Dr. Michael Beckwith is the Founder and Senior Minister of one of the world's largest and most rapidly expanding spiritual communities, the Agape International Truth Center, located in Culver City, California. A pioneering organization in the New Thought-Ancient Wisdom tradition of spirituality and philosophy, the Agape community has 7,500 members and thousands of friends worldwide.

Agape is the manifestation of Dr. Beckwith's own explorations in the emergence of consciousness. As a freshman student at Morehouse College, he was exposed to the Christian mysticism of the renowned philosopher and humanitarian, Dr. Howard Thurman. Insightful glimpses into the spiritual realm, familiar to him since childhood, were given credence and encouragement to flourish. By the time he transferred to the University of Southern California, he began to experience conscious jolts of spiritual awakening. Led to discard a traditional college curriculum, he entered a period of intense study of Eastern religion and philosophy and the practice of meditation, culminating in his enrollment in the Ernest Holmes School of Ministry, founded by the late Dr. Ernest Holmes.

Dr. Beckwith embraced an expanded identity which transcended–yet included–Western spirituality. His visionary soul-life married East and West, which today is one of the distinguishing hallmarks of his unique transdenominational Agape Center. His all-embracing approach is born of a coherent vision which honors and incorporates time-tested methods of affirmative prayer and meditation passed down from the traditions of Bhagavan Krishna, Gautama Buddha, Jesus the Christ and spiritual masters of contemporary times.

In 1986, Dr. Beckwith's inner vision revealed a world united on an ethical basis of humankind's highest development spiritually, philosophically, educationally, culturally, scientifically and socially. Applying a visioning technique originated by Dr. Beckwith, committed associates came forward to participate in his vision, resulting in the formation of the Agape International Truth Center. Now, just thirteen years later, Agape facilitates a network of twenty ministries, some of which feed the homeless, serve prisoners and their families, provide hospice and grief support, partner with community organizations and support programs which advocate the preservation of the planet's environmental resources.

Dr. Beckwith serves as National Co-director of "A Season for Nonviolence," an international movement founded in partnership with Arun Gandhi, founder of the M.K. Gandhi Institute for Nonviolence. "Season" promotes and teaches the principles of *ahimsa*, nonviolence, practiced by Mahatma Gandhi and Dr. Martin Luther King, Jr. He is also a founding member of the Association for Global New Thought, which convened "The Synthesis Dialogues" with His Holiness the Dalai Lama, in Dharmsala, India.

Thousands gather at Agape on Sundays and Wednesdays to learn from Dr. Beckwith's spiritual connection to the timeless realm, as he shares in a down-to-earth style timely truths applicable to twenty-first century living. His is a passionately unique voice, announcing to all that they are a vital, essential and beloved part of the total consciousness of the Universe.

For information about Dr. Beckwith's availability as a speaker, keynote conference speaker, retreat facilitator, or to conduct a seminar on his unique Visioning technique, please call: (310) 348-1250. Or write to:

Dr. Michael Beckwith
Agape International Truth Center
5700 Buckingham Parkway
Culver City, 90230

Agape Publishing hopes that you enjoyed this book.
If you would like to subscribe to
Rev. Dr. Michael Beckwith's sermon tapes
or the Sound of Agape performed by the Agape
International Choir, Rickie Byars and other soloists,
please contact:

Quiet Mind Bookstore
5700 Buckingham Parkway
Culver City, CA 90230
(310) 348-1266

Please visit the Agape International Truth Center Website
at: www.agapeonline.org